OECD INDUSTRIAL
RELATIONS PROGRAMME

Special Studies

Labour
Disputes

A Perspective

The Organisation for Economic Co-operation and Development (OECD) was set up under a Convention signed in Paris on 14th December 1960, which provides that the OECD shall promote policies designed:

- to achieve the highest sustainable economic growth and employment and a rising standard of living in Member countries, while maintaining financial stability, and thus to contribute to the development of the world economy;
- to contribute to sound economic expansion in Member as well as non-member countries in the process of economic development;
- to contribute to the expansion of world trade on a multilateral, non-discriminatory basis in accordance with international obligations.

The Members of OECD are Australia, Austria, Belgium, Canada, Denmark, Finland, France, the Federal Republic of Germany, Greece, Iceland, Ireland, Italy, Japan, Luxembourg, the Netherlands, New Zealand, Norway, Portugal, Spain, Sweden, Switzerland, Turkey, the United Kingdom and the United States.

TABLE OF CONTENTS

Where people work together in an employing organisation it would be expecting too much of human nature that disputes should not arise between employers and workers and for that matter between different groups of workers, and within management. This Report is mainly about those disputes which occur between employers and workers. It sets out to review, in an international perspective, the apparent trends in respect of such disputes; what problems they pose for trade unions and employers' associations, and, in particular, for public policy; and how disputes may best be avoided or resolved. It also examines the services provided by the State in respect of labour disputes and the special case where disputes bear particularly heavily on the public interest.

The Report is the product of a long-term interest in labour disputes of the OECD Working Party on Industrial Relations, developing from a decision of the OECD Council, in May 1970, concerning assessment of the volume and economic impact of disputes. This decision led to the report by Dr. Malcolm Fisher, "Measurement of Labour Disputes and their Economic Effects", published by the Organisation in 1973. Arising from consideration of that report it was decided to pursue work along two lines. Firstly, the Fisher report made it clear that national disputes statistics were commonly capable of some improvement and, on a technical level, work was carried out to that end.(1) Secondly, it was thought desirable to explore certain aspects of disputes more deeply, this leading to the commissioning of three studies.

The first of these studies, with the generous co-operation of the United Kingdom Department of Employment, was carried out by Mr. Keith Baker of that Department. It dealt with emergency disputes; i.e. those substantially and urgently affecting the well-being of a nation. The second, entrusted to Professor Gérard Adam and M. Jean-Paul Bachy, of the Conservatoire National des Arts et

---

(1) The Secretariat developed, with the help of national and international authorities, and individual experts, a set of recommendations regarding definitions and methods of data collection which would facilitate international comparability of disputes statistics.

Métiers, Paris, concerned the services afforded by the State to workers and employers involved, or potentially concerned, in disputes. The third study, carried out by Mr. Michael Shalev (now at the University of Wisconsin, Madison), dealt with trends in labour disputes.

In preparing the present Report extensive use has been made of the ideas and data presented in these three studies but while the considerable contribution made by the consultants is gratefully acknowledged they are in no way responsible for the use that has been made of their work or for the views expressed in this Report.

Before turning to more detailed consideration it may be helpful to explain the meaning attached to 'labour disputes' and the general position taken about them in this Report.

Labour disputes are conflicts of view between employers and workers. For the present purpose the term 'workers' embraces all who work under a contract or statute of employment and therefore includes managers (in their relationship with their own hierarchical superiors), professional staff, supervisors, and white-collar as well as manual workers. While the term 'dispute', as defined, covers a variety of situations the Report treats primarily with differences which are manifested by departures from normal working. Wider aspects are touched on but in the main the Report is concerned with the most common manifestation of such conflict, the strike, this in turn being taken as a withdrawal of labour intended to induce an employer, or employers, to accede to workers' wishes on an issue concerned with wages, employment, or working conditions or practices. The employers' equivalent of the strike, the lockout, is also taken into consideration but is much less used than the strike. Political strikes, i.e. strikes whose main objective is to change legislation or government policies, are not discussed.

For simplicity the strike is taken as a collective phenomenon, though the significance of individual and sectional grievance procedures as facilitating expression of conflict is taken into account. Though disputes of rights are not overlooked the emphasis is on disputes of interest.

A strike carries certain overtones in the public mind. It is sometimes regarded as rather reprehensible, particularly if it has a direct and appreciable impact on the public. Since strife is more newsworthy than peace the communications media tend to dwell on disputes but not to feature measures taken to avoid them nor the amicable resolution of differences by employers and workers. Looked at economically, of course, a strike is, amongst other things, part of the cost of a self-regulating collective bargaining system.

A telling (if not altogether acceptable) way to put the effect of strikes into perspective is to compare the working time thus lost

with the time lost over the same base period on account of sickness
or industrial accidents (some would add a comparison with the time
lost in industry through the unemployment of workers). Such comparisons make strike losses look relatively small but the misleading
element of the comparison is, of course, that in absence through
sickness or accident those at work normally do their best to ensure
the minimum disruption of production whereas to do so in a strike
(if there be any workers remaining at work) would amount to strike
breaking and defeat the normal objective of securing the strikers'
goals by causing maximum disruption of the employer's activities.

The incidence of strikes should also be put in perspective.
For instance in the United Kingdom, where fragmented strikes, i.e.
strikes by sections of a plant's labour force, are widely reputed to
be common, a Department of Employment Study of the years 1971-1973
showed that in any one year 98 per cent of plants employing approxi-
mately 80 per cent of workers had no strikes at all and most of the
remaining 20 per cent in the affected 2 per cent of plants were not
involved either directly or indirectly in the stoppages.

The Report does not consider strikes as being 'good' or 'bad'.
Its fundamental position may be summarised as:

a) That the general right to strike (or lockout) is a basic
   freedom, essential in a democratic country.
b) That that right should only be restricted where a clear need
   exists, in the public interest; in which case machinery
   should be available to ensure that those prevented from ex-
   ercising the right should have an effective alternative
   means of obtaining a speedy and equitable settlement of
   their disputes.
c) That insofar as a strike (or lockout) may bring into the
   open, and serve to dispel, long-festering grievances, or
   achieve socially and/or economically desirable improvements,
   its net result may well be more positive than negative.

These things said, the Report considers that any means which can
reasonably be adopted by employers and trade unions or, where con-
sistent with the national framework, by the State, to reduce the
volume and severity of disputes, and to find effective and less expensive alternative means of resolving them, should be encouraged.

The legal setting in which labour disputes occur varies considerably between countries. A broad division can be made between
countries like Germany, where industrial relations operate in a
framework based on the rule of law and countries like the United
Kingdom, where, though there is a considerable body of law, the in-

dustrial relations system has grown up pragmatically, regulated by the parties. Such a distinction is substantial enough to cause some confusion when international comparisons are attempted, but it does not appear to be a decisive factor in relation to the volume or obduracy of disputes and it seems feasible to treat disputes as socio-economic manifestations without seeking to disentangle the immensely complex mass of legislative acts and judicial decisions which invest the subject. Law is important in industrial relations and has both controlling and educative functions, but at root it exists to serve social and economic needs and not to be their master. Its institutions are usually responsive to changing needs. It is the needs which are considered here and accordingly the law will only be discussed insofar as it impinges on disputes in an immediate and substantive way.

The Report is also deliberately limited in another respect. It would be impossible, in a readable compass, to deal with the disputes procedures of all Member countries. The Report is therefore mainly based on the experience of a selection of countries, several of which the consultants mentioned were able to visit, though examples have been drawn from some other countries where they could illuminate a particular point. For similar reasons the Report concentrates on countries where negotiations are mainly the responsibility of unions and employers themselves, though this has prevented consideration in any depth of the interesting Australasian practice of State-provided conciliation and arbitration as an alternative to, or as supplemented by, collective bargaining.

This report has been prepared by the Secretariat for discussion by the Working Party on Industrial Relations. Given the widespread interest in industrial disputes and the means of dealing with them in Member countries the Secretary-General has thought it useful to make this document available to a wider audience.

Chapter 1

TRENDS IN LABOUR DISPUTES

Evaluation of trends in labour disputes necessarily entails consideration of both quantitative and qualitative aspects. Neither is a simple matter. On the quantitative side there are serious statistical problems and the qualitative aspects both involve subjective criteria and suffer from an adequate lack of data.

The statistical complexities have been fully discussed by Fisher[1] and need not be examined further here. The first main element of concern to the analyst is the number of strikes[2] or, to facilitate comparison, their incidence, i.e. the number of strikes related to time and to the potential striking population. This element is complicated both by the difficulty of arriving at a statistical definition of a strike or stoppage (the action may be a series of brief stoppages of work by the same workers or several actions by different, but associated, work groups; it may not be regarded as a stoppage for statistical purposes if it lasts only a few hours) and by the difficulty of deciding who is covered by the term 'potential striking population'.

Second is the number of workers involved in a strike, a concept blurred by the complication of counting those whose work cannot continue because of the strike and, again, by the difficulty of deciding what constitutes a single strike. Third, the duration of the strike is also not free from the complications mentioned. Fourth, though each of the indicators mentioned is important, perhaps the best and most readily comparable measures of severity is the volume of strikes, the number of man-days lost, which can also be related to the potential striking population. However, because of its composite nature, volume does not easily lend itself to interpretation. It may be added that in aggregations, the concepts of average size (number of strikers per strike) and average duration (number of days on strike per striker) are also used.

1) Malcom Fisher, Measurement of Labour Disputes and Their Economic Effects, OECD, Paris, 1973.
2) Though it should be pointed out that because of differences in definitions used and in methods of data collection, this is an unreliable basis for undertaking international comparison.

Yet another complicating factor is that in making comparisons the statistical weight of one particularly big strike - or perhaps two or three strikes - can easily lead to false assumptions about trends. And it is common for a tiny number of strikes to account for a high proportion of the total of both involvements and man-days lost in a country.

For some purposes one may wish to consider not only the strikers themselves but also the numbers of workers laid off as a result of the strike. Countries vary in their recording of such indirect involvements and no country seems to keep systematic records for workers affected beyond those employed in the establishment or enterprise in which the strike has occurred.

The already considerable statistical problems are intensified by variation in the accuracy of reporting, both over time and between regions or districts within countries. There is evidence for some countries (through the collection of data by more than one means) that official statistics tend to underestimate the volume of strike activity, particularly as concerns small, short and unofficial stoppages.

When it comes to inter-country comparison the many problems already mentioned are compounded, as Fisher showed in the study cited by the appreciably varying bases on which different countries compute their statistics.

Other problems include the paucity of data broken down by industry or occupation, by subject matter, by outcome, and by status - whether they are lawful, 'official' (in the sense of conforming to stipulations in union rule books), or 'constitutional', permissible in terms of agreements between unions and employers covering the situation (not to be confused with the wider political meaning of the word 'constitutional').

These inadequacies have been described in order to make clear the limitations of the data, and accordingly of inferences drawn from it. But this does not mean that no useful implications can be drawn from existing data. If, within a country, the profile of strikes changes markedly over time, or if the inter-industry patterns change, the reasons may be important. If, between countries, the 'league table' shows differences or commonalities, or if one country consistently has a preponderance of small and short strikes while another has fewer but much longer strikes, it seems worthwhile to ask why. The data are, at least, adequate for such consideration.

What the Statistics Show

At the end of the 1950s two American scholars made a thorough attempt to analyse strike trends in 15 countries (13 being OECD

countries) from 1900 to 1956.(1) They found it possible to fit
these countries into four patterns of behaviour. Five major influ-
ences were isolated as affecting strike activity: the stability of
workers' organisations; leadership conflicts within labour movements; the status of union-management relations (such as acceptance
of unions by employers and the nature of the bargaining structure);
the political affiliation of labour organisations; and the role of
the State in defining terms of employment and in disputes settlement.
The authors concluded that throughout the world strikes had been
getting shorter and could be said to be "withering away". This de-
cline of the strike they attributed to: increasingly sophisticated
policies and effective organisation amongst employers; a more active role on the part of the State; and a switch in emphasis by
the labour movement from industrial to political goals.

Ross and Hartman's work has not been without its critics,
neither as to its methodology nor its substance, and some of the
conclusions drawn have been seen to be inaccurate: certainly the
strike has not "withered away". There is no point in criticising
the findings here. They are presented as an indication of how
trends were seen by reputable authorities at the end of the fifties; as a starting point for looking at subsequent trends; and
also as a warning of the dangers of generalised prediction.

It is not possible, in the compass of this Report, to make a
statistical analysis of recent strike trends. What follows is in-
dicative rather than comprehensive: it seeks to paint a general
picture, not to present a photograph. It is based on Shalev's
analysis(2) of trends, mainly related to the years 1950 to 1972,
though some of his surveys extended over a longer period. In writ-
ing this chapter a major problem had to be faced. It was not prac-
ticable to reproduce Shalev's extensive and detailed material. In
view of the interest of the subject it has been judged necessary
to make use of Shalev's findings without presenting their full
argument.

Shalev's figures are based on relative volume, defined as days
lost per thousand persons employed in mining, manufacturing, construction and transport. This measure is less affected than others
by methodological differences in data collection and processing between countries and over time.

Most of the countries reviewed by Shalev have experienced little overall change in their position in the hierarchy, subject to

---

1) A.M. Ross and P.T. Hartman, Changing Patterns of Industrial
   Conflict, Wiley, New York, 1960.

2) M. Shalev, "Trends in Employment Conflict", unpublished study
   prepared for the OECD, 1976.

occasional deviation, over 45 years. The main exceptions have been Canada and Japan, which have risen in rank (though for Japan there were special reasons accounting for its low position before the war), and Sweden, Norway and Belgium, whose rank order has declined.

This relative stability suggests that the forces determining the volume of strike activity in a particular country are to some extent peculiar to that country, and relatively unchanging, and, secondly, that the stability of broad cross-national difference is an indication that at least some of the forces influencing the incidence of strikes over time have been common to a number of countries. A further aspect is that, even allowing for the exceptional case of the French 'évènements' of 1968, the period 1968-1972 stands out as particularly strike prone - and notably so in some of the customarily 'quiet' countries.

A significant factor underlying the number of strikes in a country is the bargaining structure. Clearly, countries with small bargaining units, a large number of collective negotiations and a high frequency of negotiations have a greater risk of strikes than others. Indeed, such countries do tend to be high in the international "league table" of strikes. In some countries a move from national to enterprise level bargaining has been accompanied by a rise in strikes.

The degree of unionisation and the breadth of the right to strike are other factors pertinent to the study of strikes.

Examination of the trends over the years 1950-1972, as analysed by Shalev(1), enable three fairly clear sub-periods to be identified. The first of these is the relatively turbulent years of the early fifties (and, had the analysis been carried back further, the late forties). This period was followed by a quite long and peaceful period (during which it could indeed seem that the strike was "withering away"), lasting nearly to the end of the 1960s. Then came a decidedly active period, heralded by the French events of 1968 and marked by the Italian 'hot autumn' and the Belgian, Dutch and German 'wildcat' strikes and the Kiruna and public service strikes in Sweden over 1969-1971.

To take the latest available figures it seems clear that the 'peaking' of 1968-1972 has passed but that strikes are remaining, generally speaking, at a significantly higher level than in the peaceful years between the early fifties and the closing years of the sixties. Given the strike figures common in pre-war days, however, it may be that it was the quiet years that were exceptional rather than the more conflictual recent years.

---

1) op. cit.

Three other comments can usefully be made from examination of the statistics. Firstly, while the number of strikes has undoubtedly shown an overall increase, it is difficult to say whether they have been becoming longer or shorter. In respect of duration there has always been a great variation between countries. In the United States, for instance, long strikes have been commonplace since the nineteenth century. In France, long strikes have been relatively uncommon and short, sometimes repeated, stoppages - rare in the United States - have been a common form. (These differences can be related to the differing institutions, union funds, practices and ethos in the industrial relations systems of the two countries). Shalev's review of the years 1950-1972 suggests that overall the mandays per involvement have been decreasing but that in nearly all countries the number of strikers per strike has been increasing.

Secondly, trends can be noted in respect of relative conflict as between particular industries and occupations. For several countries coal mining and dockwork, for instance, and construction in some countries, have been notable for a high degree of conflict over many years. In recent years this tendency has become less marked, but in the manufacturing sector metalworking has tended to assume a substantial proportion(1) and there has been a marked extension of strikes to new occupational groups. Thirdly, there has been an increase in the overall numbers of workers involved in strike action. Thus for Sweden Shalev found a more than sevenfold increase in relative involvement (that is to say involvements in strikes per 10,000 workers) between 1956-1968 and 1969-1972; also over time he found increases of around 250 per cent in Ireland and Canada; 150 per cent in Australia, Belgium, Germany, the Netherlands, New Zealand and the United Kingdom, and 50 per cent in France, Italy and the United States. It would seem that involvement in strikes has been rising over a remarkably broad front, often including branches of the economy where dispute activity was previously unknown. Shalev further found that in at least half of 13 countries examined the most extensive proportional increases were traceable to tertiary sector employees, previously very far down in the strike hierarchy. Strikes in public employment had become particularly evident in some countries where traditionally they had been low.

The Nature of Industrial Action

So far this chapter has outlined the extent and profile of one form of industrial action, the strike. There are fewer hard statistical data for tracing trends in the qualitative aspects of strikes,

1) Shalev found that over the period 1950-72 metal making/metalworking contributed between 20 per cent and 30 per cent of all work stoppages in 11 out of 13 countries examined. (Of course these industries are in any case large industries).

and other industrial action. But enough has been written about labour disputes to give some indication of the forms of action being taken and of apparent trends.

Undoubtedly the strike remains the basic form of action used in labour disputes. The employers' counter-weapon, the lockout, also remains in use, though almost everywhere it is used sparingly. Strikes are not, of course, always simple and straightforward stoppages of work. In nature as in causation the strike is a complex phenomenon. To take some broad divisions, a strike may be 'political' or 'industrial'. It may be an all-out trial of strength or a simple demonstration of discontent. It may be 'legal', 'official', 'constitutional' or the reverse of any of these.(1) It may be an action by a small group, union or non-union, intended to enforce satisfaction of an aspiration, or part of a complex battle between an employer, or a group of employers, and a union or unions. A withdrawal of labour from the establishments of an employer or group of employers may have nothing to do with the immediate employers, being intended to influence a third party. There may be a partial stoppage, whereby a number of strategically-placed workers withdraw their labour. In a widely dispersed activity like, say, a railway system, workers may stop work in different parts of the system on different days. In contrast all workers may give notice to terminate their employment at the same time.

A strike normally means the withdrawal of workers from their place of employment. But workers may have a 'sit down strike', remaining present but not working. Alternatively they may occupy the place of employment, exclude, or sequester, members of the management yet continue work. They may even take over the running of the enterprise.

The strike is not the only form of industrial action by which workers can exert pressure on their employers. They may 'work to rule' in a manner which, by adhering to the letter of often forgotten or unpractised wording, seriously impairs normal performance, or achieve a similar effect by a 'go-slow'. They may refuse to work overtime or to work at piecework tempo, or refuse certain work, or to work with certain people or tools or in a particular manner. Workers may all feel sick at the same time and stay away from work (a 'sick-out'). In at least one case a British union said that its members would work 'without enthusiasm' until their claim was met. In Japan, where trade unions are mainly based on the enterprise, identify with it, and see damage to it as harmful to their own interests, action may take the form of demonstrations outside the

---

1) Hugh Clegg has recently discussed some of the implications of these distinctions in Trade Unions under Collective Bargaining, Blackwell, Oxford, 1976, Chapter 6.

place of work to signal, by banners, headbands, etc. the workers'
dissatisfaction with their management. Lastly, industrial action
may comprise a combination of two or more of the forms described and
certainly any form of strike is likely to be accompanied by picketing of the entrances to the place of employment.

As to the way in which industrial action is carried out, in industrial relations the strike is to negotiation as in international
relations warfare is to diplomacy: the rules of intercourse are not
the same. But though tempers are likely to rise, the overwhelming
majority of industrial disputes are conducted without violence, and
almost invariably without bloodshed, and sabotage is not common.

What tendencies are apparent in the form and conduct of industrial action? As already mentioned there is little hard evidence
but it would seem from the literature that non-strike action of the
kinds described above has commonly increased more than simple strike
action. Perhaps the form of action which has more notably increased
in recent years (though the actual number of cases is still very
small) has been the occupation of the workplace leading, in some
publicised cases, to keeping open the works as a going concern, or
even to the establishment of a workers' co-operative. An occupation is likely to involve breach of law but this has rarely been made
an issue of the dispute though the police have not uncommonly been
called on to eject workers from the premises. Occupations appear to
have had most impact where the issue involved has been the intended
closure of the enterprise, or some part thereof, where local opinion
may strongly support the workers (especially if there is little other
work available locally) and wider public opinion is likely to be
torn between the Scylla of increasing unemployment and its costs to
the public purse, and the Charybdis of continuing what may prove a
very unprofitable operation.

Lastly, reference should be made to the possibility of trans-
nationalisation of disputes. Naturally the growth of operations of
multinational enterprises has increased the possibility of conflict
between a union and employer in one country coming to involve a
union and the same employer in another country. Up to the present
there have been very few such cases but the growth of multinational
enterprises and the closer liaison instituted within international
trade union organisations suggest that more of them may be encountered in the future, perhaps particularly in the form of threatened
boycott of goods produced in another country for the enterprise involved in a dispute. Additionally, should transnational collective
bargaining develop, as has been discussed within the framework of
the European Economic Community, there would clearly be a further potentiality for transnational disputes.

What of the issues underlying labour disputes? The 'staple'
remains, as at almost all times and in almost all countries, pay:
being the main issue in probably at least half of the disputes and
more if other disputes in which pay is an underlying factor are included. Otherwise, prevailing issues vary according to circumstances. For example, in times of depression a particularly high
priority is naturally accorded by unions to saving jobs. Conversely,
as industrial relations systems become more highly developed there
are likely to be fewer cases concerning union recognition.

Though again with little hard quantitative evidence, it is undoubtedly true, at least for many countries, that the issues in
disputes have been widening as the employment relationship has become more complex. Through social improvement there are now more
elements in the relationship to dispute about (sick pay, pensions,
etc.). Technological change has brought forward new issues.
Additionally, many elements traditionally regarded as within the
prerogative of management have increasingly come to be challenged —
as indeed has the whole traditional philosophy of management
rights.(1) Workers have always been prepared to fight speed-ups,
or the introduction of what they regard as undesirable labour, but
today, at least in some countries, many acts of management are likely
to be met by a threat of industrial action.

The widening issues at the workplace, and the accompanying
trend, in some countries, for the locus of collective bargaining to
move towards the enterprise or workplace(2) has also affected
control by official union leadership of rank and file action, the
rank and file tending to take more responsibility in disputes.

One important gradual change in the subject matter of disputes
should also be noted. For many years now governments' responsibilities for economic policy have made it difficult for most of them to
ignore trends in the movement of wage levels. Under the inflation-
ary yet recessionary conditions which became common in 1974 governments have tended to involve themselves more and more in formulating
some kind of norm or limit for wage increases. This has naturally
had an effect on wage bargaining at lower levels and has increased
the danger of almost overall conflict in the event of trade union
leadership and government being unable to reach agreement on the desirable course to follow.

---

1) As already mentioned, this Report excludes matters which are
normally outside the scope of the employment relationship but
even provision of community facilities has been negotiated in
Italy.

2) See N.F. Dufty, Changes in Labour-Management Relations in the
Enterprise, OECD, Paris, 1975.

Lastly, are strikes becoming more expensive and, if so, to whom and in what terms? There is not enough data to show, though it might be thought that the ever-increasing capital intensivity and organisational integration of industry, and in some countries the increase in public monopoly, would make them so. In fact it is extremely difficult to estimate the cost of disputes, be it to employer, workers, or the community.(1) Obviously all strikes have costs to each of these parties, even though these may be offset by still less tangible gains. Such work as has been done on costs(2) suggests that they are commonly over-estimated and it is apparent that to measure costs in terms of sales value of potential product loss, as is commonly done, is usually misleading. Other work(3) suggests that support to strikers and/or their families, in some countries, through State social security and similar allowances, is not critical in decisions to strike or to continue a strike.

Causes underlying present trends in labour disputes

The most significant apparent trends in labour disputes identified in this Report have been that, 'peaks' apart, there has been a fairly generalised but modest rise in the volume of strike activity; that the subject matter of disputes has been widening out; that the 'striking population' has come to include many more workers, including many new groups; and that there has been some shift within unions towards the rank and file leadership having greater control over their disputes. Each of these subjects calls for further comment but first something may usefully be said on the broader question of volume of disputes.

How should movement of the general level of strike activity be regarded? Firstly it is necessary to distinguish between underlying trends and movements caused by particular - and not necessarily enduring - combinations of circumstances, perhaps partly national and partly affecting several countries. An illustration of the latter is the strike wave which, as already described, hit several European countries around 1968 to 1971, including some with good records of industrial peace. There is no single simple explanation of this phenomenon(4) but the causes would seem to be partly the sudden

1) For a review of the economic problems involved see Fisher, op.cit.
2) Notably in the United States where careful studies have been made of strikes in the steel industry and in docks and railways.
3) See articles in British Journal of Industrial Relations, March and November 1974.
4) The experience has been fully discussed in G. Spitaels (ed), Les Conflits Sociaux en Europe, Marabout, Brussels, 1971, and more recently, in S. Barkin (ed), Worker Militancy and its Consequences, 1965-75, Praeger, New York, 1975.

crystallising of a number of deep-seated social and economic changes, of the kind discussed below; partly that some wage increases had been negotiated on the basis of over-pessimistic growth forecasts, so that workers felt deprived in relation to the unexpected prosperity enjoyed by employers; and partly that after long industrial peace both some union leaderships and employers had failed to note, and act upon, changing attitudes at the workplace.

Special phenomena apart, and allowing for the recent overall fall in strike volume,(1) reflecting present economic imperatives, the statistics and such underlying factors as appear from analysis give no reason to suppose that the long spell of relative industrial peace enjoyed by many countries in the fifties and sixties is likely to return. The forces at work suggest more future industrial tension rather than less. It is now necessary to consider, briefly, what these forces are.

One group concerns the attitudes which people bring to their work.(2) People at work are better educated than they used to be - and increasingly education has taught them to question rather than conform to authority. At least until recently, most members of the labour force had grown up against a background of - certainly by pre-war standards - full employment, which enhanced their self-confidence and bargaining power. The protection afforded by the safety net of the welfare state has also contributed to workers' feeling of security. And almost continuous economic growth has bred expectations of steady improvement in standards of living. (The check to such expectations enforced by the recent economic situation has naturally itself produced some tensions: that these have not been greater than they have is attributable to workers' common-sense realisation of the limitations on what can be achieved, coupled, of course, with the improved provisions for income maintenance and social security which have become common in many countries).

Against these attitudinal factors must be set changes at the place of work. There, technological and economic change since the war, and the organisational changes that have accompanied them, have increased in rapidity. Such changes have two consequences. Firstly, change in itself is likely to be disturbing, particularly if, as has not uncommonly been the case, it threatens one's livelihood. Secondly, changes such as computerisation and the increasing ease of global travel have made it easier to exercise centralised control, often seen by rank and file workers as impersonal.

An increase in the size of multinational operations, and of workplaces generally, has also made for distance between those who

1) As shown by the ILO Year Book of Labour Statistics, 1976.
2) A relevant analysis is contained in R.W. Revans, The Emerging Attitudes and Motivation of Workers, OECD, Paris, 1972.

make major decisions and those they affect, with accompanying misunderstanding. Lastly, as already noted, industry has become more capital intensive and closely integrated, and therefore more vulnerable to industrial action (though, at the same time, where an enterprise is highly automated the employer may find it easier to maintain operations through the use of managerial and supervisory personnel.)

Obviously the effects of these two sets of trends run counter to each other. Higher expectations and greater industrial strength amongst workers are in a framework of disturbance and greater potentiality for misunderstanding. Except for the constraints which recent economic difficulties and their associated higher levels of unemployment have added to the scene, there seems no reason to suppose that the discordant factors reviewed above are going to wane and it is reasonable to conclude that tensions are likely to increase rather than lessen in employment relations in industrial societies.

Further comment needs to be made about general levels of disputes. This Report posited at the outset that some degree of conflict was inevitable in our societies. What degree might be said to be normal? There is no straight answer to this question - what level is acceptable will be a reflection of the political and economic framework of each particular society at the particular time. The only generalisation which can be offered is the rather obvious one that if the disruption to society generally is great enough decisively to outweigh the considerable importance which should be attached to the freedom of employers and unions to take economic measures against each other, as well as to talk, it is desirable to enquire into the circumstances and to consider what ameliorative steps can be taken and (with caution) whether changes in law are necessary. But the fact that, for particular reasons, the level of disputes in a country has come to be higher than in the past, or is higher than that in a comparable country, is not of itself necessarily alarming.

The broadening of the subject matter of collective bargaining and hence of disputes seems to be a natural development, mirroring other trends in society, notably the trend to greater participation by ordinary people in decisions that affect them. Insofar as the subject matter has come to include decisions on the general conduct of the enterprise, long considered as 'managerial prerogatives', it may seem that attention needs to be paid to the effects of disputes on ultimate operational efficiency. It is one thing for an enterprise to be forced by industrial action to pay higher wages: it may be another for such action to compel an enterprise to adopt inefficient production methods. However, these are matters which involve differing views of social priorities, and differing value systems, which are too complex to analyse here.

The extension of the 'strike prone population' is also a natural enough development. The causes of tension discussed above affect many groups beyond those traditionally associated with strikes. White collar workers have commonly felt pressed towards action by what they see as erosion of traditional advantages compared with manual workers, and by the sight of manual workers achieving gains by industrial action which they have not been granted. Public employees have been affected by similar experiences but also by the considerable growth and increasing heterogeneity of public employment in nearly all countries. Almost all groups in our societies have felt it necessary to consider how they can hold their own relative position when they see traditionally organised bargaining groups keeping pace with - or outpacing - inflation. And a great many groups have both sensed possession of greater strength in the bargaining situation and felt greater confidence in using it.

The main problems posed by the extension of the strike prone population are (a) the inexperience of some of the groups and employers newly embarking on collective bargaining and (b) for public employees, particularly civil servants covered by statute rather than contract, the propriety of disputes with a sovereign government.

Next, it has become obvious that in a number of European countries there has been a shift in levels of collective bargaining- indeed of industrial relations activity generally - in the postwar years. In a few cases increased weight has come to be placed on a central national bargain, even apart from the extent to which the central national level has come to be the forum for discussion of wage movements in relation to national economic policy. More commonly, however, added weight has accrued at the enterprise or workplace level.(1)

From the point of view of labour disputes two things are apparent in respect of the increased importance of the enterprise level. Firstly, it is often considered desirable to work out a satisfactory solution to a dispute between people who themselves have to work under that solution, as opposed to working under a possibly more general and less appropriate settlement made at a higher level. So far so good, but secondly, if individual managements and workers are to regulate wages and working conditions it becomes much more difficult, in countries used to national or regional bargaining, to keep the situation in the enterprise within nationally desirable guidelines and to maintain the authority customarily belonging to national and local trade union and employers' association officials. Such loss of authority may be reflected in increased unofficial action.

---

1) See N.F. Dufty, op. cit.

Trade unions tending to be so much larger and more complex than employers' associations the problem of authority has usually been particularly apparent in terms of trade union structure and policy. In fact, trade unions in the countries concerned have done much to overcome the problem of integrating what happens within the enterprise with the wider industrial relations system. Measures have been worked out with employers for an orderly articulation of the various levels of collective bargaining, as in Sweden. Steps have been taken to improve communications with the rank and file, and to step up trade union education. National union leaders have adapted their role to changing circumstances. There is good reason to suppose that developments of these kinds, where changes necessitate them, will come about naturally. Nevertheless, one misunderstanding continues to recur in respect of trade union leadership. It is not uncommon, in some countries, to find union leaders castigated by employers and in newspaper articles for not ensuring that their members honour a procedure agreement or accept terms of settlement to which union leaders are prepared to agree. The misunderstanding rests on the fallacious view of a union as an army under the control of officers. Of course an efficient union will have a good rapport between leadership and led and a measure of internal discipline, and of course employers (and society) are entitled to expect union leaders to exercise reasonable authority and responsibility, but basically a trade union is a voluntary and a democratic organisation: its members make its policy and its leaders (often subject to popular election) are put in their positions to carry out, as much as to inspire, the courses of action decided by the union's policy-making bodies.

Chapter 2

AVOIDANCE AND RESOLUTION OF DISPUTES
AND THE SERVICES OF THE STATE

As explained in the preface this Report takes for granted that some degree of conflict is inevitable in employing organisations. But it also considers that few people want to live in an atmosphere of conflict: workers do not want to lose their wages nor employers their production. Nor do the public want to do without goods and services which they need. There is therefore good reason to find non-disruptive means of dealing with differences between employers and workers.

The evolution of peaceful means of avoiding, channelling and resolving conflict is a mark of a developed democracy. The more that unions and employers can build and operate such machinery themselves(1) the better: in the area of labour disputes, apart from the legislature establishing the ground rules, the role of the State is mainly a supplementary and supportive one.

The present chapter notes the main forms evolved by employers and unions to deal with conflict and examines the role of the State and the forms of public assistance and control practised. It draws heavily on the Report(2): "The Services of the State in the Resolution of Labour Disputes" prepared for the OECD by Professor Gérard Adam and Mr. Jean-Paul Bachy of the Conservatoire national des arts et métiers, Paris.

Private Means of Avoiding or Resolving Disputes

It is almost a tautology to say that the greatest single contribution to avoiding disputes within the enterprise is by good managerial industrial relations practices. These practices, which cannot be detailed here, show little variation between countries.

---

1) Though joint procedures are usual, unions or employers may have their own internal procedures. Both union rules and those of employers' associations commonly include provisions governing conduct in the event of disputes. There has recently been a tendency for Italian unions to work out their own rules for collective action.

2) Prepared in 1976. Unpublished.

Turning to the wider industrial relations systems in OECD countries, the variation is still so great as to make categorisation difficult, but three broad types can be distinguished on a basis which has implications for examining labour disputes. These may be described as 'consensual', 'conflictual' and 'limited conflictual'.

Consensual systems may be exemplified by the Scandinavian countries, West Germany, Austria and Switzerland. To call such systems consensual does not imply identity of viewpoint between employers, workers and governments - they may have deep differences apart from disagreeing on wages and similar matters - but does assume that there is broad agreement about the nature and goals of the industrial relations system and of the wider society.

In conflictual systems - Italy is an example - the whole range of subjects of mutual concern to employers and workers may be regarded as potentially disputable, to be mediated, where desired, through a bargaining process. 'Conflictual' does not imply that employers and workers are always at odds; that there are no areas of agreement: it is a question of degree. Equally it is not intended to suggest that conflictual systems are 'bad' and consensual ones 'good'. Many people dislike the idea of conflict but for most purposes the result yielded is more important than the approach to its mediation.

In the limited conflictual systems, typified by the United States, employers and unions are in the main in agreement that over a defined area - that of collective bargaining - their relationship is an antagonistic one, but that in other areas they have common interests and even in the 'antagonistic' area they have the will to resolve conflict on the basis of agreed rules.

An implication of this categorisation is that one would expect the level of disputes to be low in consensual countries and high in conflictual and limited conflictual countries - as proves broadly to be the case. But further, it is reasonable to assume that in the consensual system there is less need for State action than in conflictual systems. In the limited conflictual systems the role of the State is likely to be most concerned with the defined area of antagonism.

The extrapolation of this crude categorisation towards evaluating the possible links between the nature of the industrial relations system and the economic and social progress of societies is beyond the scope of this Report. Equally the detailed examination of different private national institutions and practices for avoiding and resolving disputes cannot be encompassed here, though it may be said that clearly there is no single model procedure, since so much depends on the particular industrial relations system and the structure of its trade unions and employers' associations. Nevertheless, two general aspects should be commented upon here, namely, the possible use of arbitration and the relevance of a 'peace' obligation in a procedure agreement.

The intention of those who make agreements to deal with disputes is to substitute a process of rational argument for the exercise of force. When the procedure laid down has run its course industrial action, compromise, or acceptance of one party's view are an open choice for the parties. The strike is a natural extension of the collective bargaining process. But apart from the possibility of using facilities provided by the State, to be discussed below, in some countries there can be recourse to private arbitration.

Arbitration

The practice of arbitration, in labour disputes as in other fields of conflict, is a very old one. Some countries have used it regardless of the nature of the impasse to be overcome. Others limit its use, notably to disputes of rights rather than disputes of interest, that is to say, disputes concerning the interpretation of an existing agreement as opposed to disputes for which few guidelines or other criteria may exist.

The form the arbitration takes may vary in several ways. There may be a single arbitrator or a group. (In the mid-nineteenth century in Britain it was common practice to submit sectional or district claims to a board of arbitration drawn from employers and trade union leaders in the industry concerned). It may differ as between arbitrators being required to give reasons for their decisions or simply announcing them, as between employing permanent arbitrators or selecting them ad hoc, or as between the parties committing themselves or not committing themselves in advance to accepting the arbitration decision. Where a group of issues are involved the arbitrator may be required to give a single award for the whole group or permitted to arbitrate each issue separately.

The practice of private arbitration is most highly developed in the United States, where it is in common use, at least for dealing with rights disputes and disciplinary cases. Ninety-five per cent of collective agreements have been said to make provision for arbitration where the parties cannot agree on interpretation. Though the outcome of American arbitration is clearly generally satisfactory (if it were not the practice would be discontinued) it is not without its critics, who are mainly concerned with the delay and expense involved but are also sometimes critical of the wisdom of some of the decisions made.

Arbitration is not a purely judicial process. The arbitrator has to find a settlement which is acceptable to the parties; one with which they can live - a process which does not disregard equity but which has sometimes been called "giving the lion's share to the lion".

A vexed issue of arbitration is whether the arbitrator should be mindful of the public interest. The parties to the dispute might well prefer that he should settle the case solely on the evidence they put before him but an arbitrator may feel himself unable to ignore, for instance, a government pronouncement on wages if he is arbitrating a case involving wages.

Given the range of existing institutions in Member countries and the present relatively small use of private arbitration in most of them it is difficult to argue for extension of the practice. Nevertheless, arbitration remains an instrument which should at least be considered, in the light of the particular national framework, when unions and employers are reviewing their arrangements for resolving disputes, not only for disputes of rights but also for disputes of interest.

The Peace Obligation

In several countries the preservation of peace between employers and unions is required by law while a contract is in force, but as treated here the peace obligation is something agreed between the parties.

It is a common feature of procedure agreements that the parties bind themselves not to take industrial action while the procedure is being followed to resolve a difference between them and/or during the life of a particular agreement. In its earliest days such a clause sometimes reflected a price paid by unions for their acceptance by employers as a bargaining partner but in any case it represents agreement that rational discussion through institutionalised procedures is superior to the law of the jungle.

In some notable cases the pattern for future peace was laid following periods of strife, as in the Basic Agreement (the Saltsjöbaden Agreement) in Sweden in 1938 and the Peace Agreement in the Swiss engineering and metal industries, signed in 1937.

An interesting example of a relatively recent industrial peace agreement is the arrangement built into the 1974 negotiations between the United Steelworkers of America and the Basic Steel Industry in the United States, and renewed in 1977, providing that while the union should retain the right to strike on unresolved local issues the parties would use final and binding arbitration for unresolved bargaining issues in the main contract negotiations.

The pattern of adherence varies but the shift in several countries from the industry to the workplace level makes peace clauses in industry-wide agreements more difficult to observe within enterprises. There is commonly, in practice, some indulgence by employers towards such breaches, particularly where they are short and may be in reaction to some ill-considered managerial action. Even where, as in Belgium, the unions guarantee industrial peace in certain important industries such as mechanical, metal and electrical construction, and benefit on this ground by a relatively high bonus payment, which may be reduced according to the number and duration of wildcat strikes(1), the overall joint analysis of industrial relations made at the end of each year generally leads the employers' organisations to waive the sanctions provided by the relevant agreement.

The Role of the State

In this Report the voluntary arrangements made by employers and unions to preserve social peace have only been commented upon to give perspective to the role of the State, which is the main focus of attention here.

A society in which employers and workers are always able to resolve their differences without disruption to others or fundamental damage to themselves is an unrealistic prospect. In fact the State has long accepted disputes as of national concern - as early as the 1850s the British Parliament debated the setting up of joint conciliation committees on a trade and district basis. Gradually the State came to take an increasing interest in labour-management conflict and now, though the approach and extent vary widely between countries, there are many ways in which governmental or independent public agencies endeavour to avoid or settle industrial conflict. Again, this report is concerned with the executive/administrative rather than the judicial approach to disputes and it is not necessary to do much more than note the work of the Labour Courts, Conseils de Prud'hommes, Industrial Tribunals and Labor Relations Boards, which usually deal with individual disputes and/or the application or interpretation of laws or collective agreements. Little criticism seems to be made of the work of such bodies in the OECD countries in which they are used. (This Report will not attempt to review the special and complex role of the quasi-judicial Australian Conciliation and Arbitration Commission).

The role of the State in respect of labour disputes may be considered as falling within the following framework:

    a) Assisting the parties by information, advice, research and educational services.

---

1) Strikes where action is taken without the conciliation procedure and the notice provided therein having been followed.

b) Providing conciliation, mediation and arbitration services for voluntary use by the parties.
c) Setting up inquiries to make the circumstances of disputes known to the public.
d) Providing compulsory conciliation, mediation and arbitration services.
e) Requiring ballots to be held before strikes take place.
f) Requiring a 'cooling-off period' before strikes take place.
g) Forceful intervention, including:
    i) seizing and operating the enterprise in dispute;
    ii) conscripting the workers concerned into public service and requiring them to carry on work;
    iii) using the armed forces to carry on the strikers' work;
    iv) legislating terms to settle the dispute.
h) Ensuring suitable arrangements for dealing with disputes in which it is involved as employer.
i) Legislating a framework, as may conform to national circumstances, for industrial relations as a whole.

The legal framework of industrial relations systems is too big and complex a subject to be treated here and items (e) to (g) are mainly concerned with the particularly serious disputes to be considered in Chapter 3, but the other elements are reviewed in the present chapter.

Information, Advice, Research and Education

In many countries the State does not have any substantial role in respect of information, advice, research and education bearing on the avoidance or resolution of labour disputes, except, of course, in preparing and publicising new legislation and in the general sense that statistics gathered by the State are a staple input to industrial negotiations. Some countries, however, have built up extensive services and programmes in this area over the years. As long ago as the 1940s the United Kingdom Ministry of Labour and National Service established an advisory team whose services were freely made available to industry. Probably most OECD countries conduct, and contract out, a certain amount of research which has a bearing on disputes.

Public financial support for education specifically concerned with labour relations has been less marked, though the subject is dealt with in public adult education programmes in a number of countries. Australia has established special trade union training facilities and the United Kingdom has assured funding of programmes for training workers' representatives. Canada has recently made

funds available to unions to establish labour education programmes
and proposes to establish a tripartitely-administered "Collective
Bargaining Information Centre", to make relevant information avail-
to employers and workers' organisations.

The assumption underlying the kind of service described is that
the investment will 'pay off' in terms of better understanding of
the bases of industrial relations and the smoother working of the
industrial relations system.

Conciliation, Mediation and Arbitration Services

The borderlines between conciliation, mediation and arbitration are often hard to draw but broadly the terms may be said to
signify:

Conciliation - where a third party serves as an impartial coun-
sellor to the employer(s) and workers in dispute, and as a go-
between. He will seek new avenues which might lead to settlement
but though he may suggest possible compromises he will not make firm
proposals as to the terms of agreement.

Mediation - where an impartial third party goes beyond conciliation to draw up firm proposals for settlement.

Arbitration - where an impartial third party considers arguments presented by the parties, then announces his award - which
may or may not be accompanied by his reasoning and may or may not
be binding on the parties.

The considerable variety of conciliation, mediation and arbitration services offered by the State, and the different views taken
of giving such services, are best illustrated by some examples,
which will necessarily also indicate how public and private services
complement each other. Except where enterprise bargaining is usual
the outlines given mainly relate to the higher levels of collective
bargaining. As throughout this Report, judicial forms of procedure
for dealing with individual grievances are not covered.

Thus, for Belgium a complex system of interlocking national-
central and national-industrial joint bodies of unions and employer
representatives, with the Chairmanship and Secretariat provided by
the State, is the most prominent element in the collective regula-
tion of relations between the parties, which are close and prag-
matic. The preferred procedures for dealing with disputes are the
most flexible and least restrictive (employers and unions alike are
decidedly opposed to arbitration and refuse it on principle). Most
joint commissions have a five-member joint conciliation bureau,
chaired by a civil servant. If the parties fail to agree it is up
to the chairman to propose a solution, though his proposal is not
binding on them. This system means that the State is represented

at all the higher stages of the bargaining process. The state representatives are drawn from a special department of the Ministry of Labour whose members have high rank and considerable autonomy: they may intervene in disputes on their own initiative or at the request of the parties to the dispute.

In Canada, collective bargaining is highly decentralised, partly because of the divided jurisdiction in labour relations. Negotiations are usually conducted between local management and the local union, although there is a trend towards broader-based bargaining. In the event of negotiations breaking down there are various systems of intervention which the governments might adopt to resolve disputes. Most Departments of Labour have mediation, conciliation and arbitration services. The unique feature of Canadian labour relations is that of compulsory conciliation before resorting to a strike or lock-out; this allows for a cooling-off period before an actual dispute takes place. Conciliation may be by a single conciliator, a conciliation board or conciliation commissioner. These do not make judgements, but submit reports to the relevant departments at the end of their proceedings, and only after these reports have been submitted can disputes be called. Mediation services are also available and may be used before or after conciliation; in most instances mediation follows conciliation. (During the period 1970 to 1974, of the agreements covering 500 employees or more (excluding those in construction), 39 per cent were settled as a result of negotiations, 26 per cent after conciliation, 6 per cent after mediation, 6 per cent after arbitration and 13 per cent after work stoppage.) In addition to these processes, the use of an Industrial Inquiry Commission is sometimes used for disputes of special importance. In case the above seems too schematic, it should be said that the federal Canada Labour Code's methods of interventions, (conciliators, conciliation boards and commissioners, mediators and industrial inquiry commissions) can be used singly and jointly, promptly or over a prolonged period, thus allowing for cooling-off.

In Denmark trade unions and employers are strongly organised, with considerable authority vested in their central bodies. There is a long-standing preference for the parties settling their own disputes. Centralisation has led to a specific timetable being adopted for central national wage negotiations. A clear distinction is made between disputes of rights and disputes of interests. An Industrial Court deals with disputes over the interpretation of agreements; breaches of agreements, and irregularities in calling strikes; it is not concerned with the substantive issues in dispute. A National Conciliation Board employs a staff of conciliators/mediators who can intervene directly or on invitation in disputes and

can ask to attend meetings of negotiating committees. They can put
forward mediation proposals and have them put to the vote. If a
dispute is of national importance the mediator can order a limited
postponement of a stoppage of work. A feature of Danish industrial
relations has been the mutual acceptance of strict bargaining procedures, with explicit circumscription of the right to strike -
penalties being exacted for strikes outside the specified bounds.
In 1973, however, a liberalisation provided that strikes not concerned with the central or an associated agreement could legiti-
mately take place if they lasted no longer than two days (repeated
short stoppages are not protected), and that in any case the Industrial Court should not impose fines on one party taking action if
the other party had behaved culpably. The Court's jurisdiction was
widened at the same time. Meanwhile, under a new Basic Agreement
of 1973, unions and employers agreed that in the event of a dispute
in an enterprise a meeting between the parties should take place
between the parties not later than the day following a stoppage.

In contrast, in France the State has been the prime mover in
promoting procedures for resolving disputes. State intervention has
taken many forms. The law, for instance, requires the parties to
include conciliation provisions in their agreements and to submit
an unresolved dispute to an arbitration procedure. Where there is
no specified conciliation body, or where sectoral boundaries are
crossed, a dispute may be dealt with through a statutory procedure
of tripartite national and regional conciliation boards. However,
in fact, out of an average of roughly 3,500 reported disputes a year
between 1950 and 1974 only 85 went through this statutory procedure.
Arbitration generally is viewed with suspicion and mediation; though
quite well received when it was instituted in 1955, it is not much
used. In practice the main agent of state involvement in disputes
is the labour inspector whose principal function, as in other countries, is ensuring observance of protective and other labour legislation. The Labour Code provides for collective labour disputes to
be notified to the Prefect, who, with the labour inspector, should
then intervene. In practice the State - through various channels -
commonly intervenes in disputes of some importance.

Germany, has, since the war, followed a strong conviction that
disputes are for unions and employers themselves to sort out, in an
orderly manner. Though the law expects a high standard of conduct
by the parties there are no legal provisions for Federal conciliation and arbitration. Only Law No 35 on Conciliation and Arbitration Procedures for Labour Disputes, of 20th August, 1946, is still
in force. It has been abrogated and replaced by provisions deviating
from it only in the Land of Rhineland-Palatinate and in the area
of South Baden, in the present Land of Baden-Würtemberg. The
Constitution of the Federal Republic has no provisions regulating

conciliation and arbitration. However, in Article 9, it does guarantee workers and employers the right to form associations and to conclude collective agreements. This includes the right to conciliation and arbitration through agreements with the opposite party. Länder Constitutions commonly have provisions for mediation. The parties, nationally, did agree, in 1954, a standard form of procedure for settling disputes. To give an example of its present application from the metalworking industry, if the parties cannot agree they have three days in which they may jointly refer the dispute to a conciliation board, which is in general composed of one neutral chairman with voting rights, one non-voting neutral chairman and two assistant members with voting rights from each party. If the parties do not jointly appeal to the conciliation board, this board can be appealed to unilaterally by either party within a further delay of two working days. The parties undertake not to go on strike or to lock out as long as the collective negotiations or the conciliation procedure are going on. An arbitration commission can be established for settling all disputes arising from the conciliation and arbitration agreement for the metalworking industry; this commission takes action upon the initiative of one party and it is entitled to impose fines for premeditated or grossly negligent violation of the conciliation and arbitration agreement. For such disputes appeal to the labour courts is excluded (the labour courts in relation to collective disputes basically deal with disrupted contract terms, alleged illegalities and the interpretation of collective agreements). Strictly there is no national conciliation, mediation or arbitration service, though clearly government does not fail to take an interest in disputes which might seriously affect the public interest. But the administrative apparatus of the state is less involved in dealing with labour disputes than is the case in most other OECD countries: (it might be added that the volume of disputes is also amongst the lowest in OECD countries).

The United Kingdom has a particularly long history of state services in relation to disputes and over the years a battery of means of assisting unions and employers to resolve their disputes has been built up. In recent years changing legislation and the exigencies of incomes policies have changed names and the shapes of institutions but the changes have increased the options rather than decreased them. The term 'mediation' has not been much used in the United Kingdom but conciliation by government officials is of very long standing, as is assistance in providing arbitrators on request. Compulsory arbitration of disputes has been applied in wartime and its aftermath, and subsequently an option to use an Industrial Disputes Tribunal issuing a binding award lasted until 1959. A Commission on Industrial Relations was set up in 1969 with

31

a variety of responsibilities, including enquiring into the circumstances of particular disputes, but was disbanded in 1974 when a new body - the Advisory, Conciliation and Arbitration Service (ACAS) under the tripartite control of employers, unions and independents - was set up, independently of the Department of Employment, to encompass most of the State's services in the field, with a general duty to promote improvement of industrial relations and the particular duty of encouraging the extension of collective bargaining and the reform of collective bargaining machinery. There is also a Central Arbitration Committee dealing with complaints under certain recognition and disclosure procedures and arbitrating in other disputes referred to it.

In the United States there are two principal national public bodies concerned with mediation, conciliation and arbitration. One is the Federal Mediation and Conciliation Service (F.M.C.S.), whose role is to help the parties to a dispute reach a settlement. It may proffer its services, either upon its own motion or upon the request of one or more of the parties to the dispute, whenever in its judgement such dispute threatens to cause a substantial interruption of commerce. The other major institution with similar responsibilities is the National Mediation Board, whose jurisdiction extends to the railway and airline industries.

Other Intervention by the State

Education and information, conciliation, mediation and arbitration have been discussed above; the more interventionist forms of state involvement in disputes are normally those used where a dispute appears so grave in its effects on the life of the nation as to necessitate intervention, more fittingly discussed in the next chapter.

Chapter 3

DISPUTES SERIOUSLY AFFECTING THE WELL-BEING OF A NATION

The services made available by the State for helping unions and
employers to resolve their disputes are offered on the rationale
that their cost is likely to be lower than the economic and social
costs that would be incurred if the services were not available.
Naturally such economic and social costs vary considerably but they
may be so great that the government is impelled to intervene, in the
public interest, whether or not one or all of the parties directly
concerned request state intervention.

A withdrawal of labour of any kind is almost certain to affect
third parties and not merely the employer(s) and workers concerned.
Indeed, strikers may wish to maximise the effect of their action on
the general public as a means of attracting attention to their
grievances and bringing pressure to bear towards a speedy settlement. But inconvenience to third parties is part of the necessary
price to be paid for the freedom to strike and lock out.

Nevertheless other basic social aspects also have to be considered. For instance, is it tolerable that society should be in-
definitely deprived of goods or services it needs because of the
obduracy of employers and/or workers? Can society allow an appar-
ently trivial cause of dispute to paralyse its normal life? Cannot such disputes be resolved in just fashion by arbitration or some
other objective formula? Have not governments, responsible for the
well-being of their countries, a special duty to help to avoid or
resolve such disputes and perhaps to ensure provision of at least
basic goods and services?

As long ago as the first decade of the century Australia established what is now the Commonwealth Conciliation and Arbitration
Commission and it is significant that a founding-father of the
Australian system, H.B. Higgins, in 1922, entitled a book setting
out its philosophy, "A New Province for Law and Order", basing his
argument on the premise that labour disputes in a civilised democratic society should be resolved in both a just and an orderly
fashion.

In practice Member countries generally have come to terms with these problems by (a) prohibiting strikes by certain work groups by law, sometimes offering alternative means of resolution of issues so that the workers concerned do not suffer for inability to use their industrial strength, (b) by public examination of the circumstances of the disputes and (c) by direct intervention in particular disputes.

Specific exclusions from the right to strike are to be found as early as the 1870s. The groups commonly so specified have included workers in services such as water, electricity and gas supply; police and firemen; and workers in postal or transportation services. Even today, in many countries some or all of these services are considered essential to the well-being of the nation and there are frequently restrictions placed on the ability of either party to interrupt them.

Some important questions about disputes which are serious to society cannot be dealt with here. Thus it is not intended to go into the complex and technical area of the general right to strike; nor the legitimacy of general strikes or of strikes with political objectives. Basically what is considered here is when, and on what grounds, governments need to intervene in a dispute and secondly the possible means of intervention.

Criteria for Intervention

When and on what grounds government should intervene are clearly judgemental matters, likely to be treated differently in countries with differing social, legal, and political frameworks and traditions. There can be no absolute yardstick: much will depend on the particular circumstances and even the views of successive governments within the same country are likely to differ. There is, however, virtual acceptance of two principles as basic in peacetime: firstly, the general right to strike is fundamental in OECD Member countries, and, secondly, excepting countries which have adopted a semi-judicial process for regulating wages and working conditions, it is considered better for employers and workers to resolve their disputes themselves than to have settlements thrust upon them.

Interventions may only really be said to occur at the point at which governments attempt conciliation. Merely making services available to the disputants on a voluntary basis cannot be said to infringe the autonomy of the parties, unless it be considered that the option thus afforded saps the resolution of the parties to settle their own disputes. For a government, provision of supportive services is mainly a matter of costs versus benefits; to intervene in a dispute of some importance, on the other hand, demands

consideration, and to intervene forcefully, most mature consideration.
At least four possible criteria for intervention can be outlined.

- First, is the dispute gravely affecting the health or safety
  of the community or seriously endangering the economy?
- Second, do the economic and social costs of the particular
  dispute to society clearly and decisively outweigh the importance of the basic principles of free collective bargaining?
- Third, is intervention desirable to ensure that the strong do
  not take undue advantage of the weak; that a reasonable degree
  of social justice prevails?
- Fourth, is intervention likely to resolve the dispute effec-
  tively? (In some cases intervention could do more harm than
  good: in particular the possibility of mass refusal by strikers
  to return to work on terms thought reasonable by those
  intervening).

Of these criteria the first, though gravity or seriousness may
be a matter of opinion, seems to be followed in most OECD countries.
The second is more dependent on national factors, but seems to offer
a commonsense basis for intervention. The third criterion, for most
OECD countries, assuming the dispute to be lawful, does not seem to
justify more than diplomatic intervention and public enquiry into,
and exposition of the facts. The proper remedy in such cases would
seem to lie in review of protective legislation or of the legal
framework of bargaining procedure. The fourth criterion is a purely
practical one.

Another question for consideration is whether intervention in
'emergency' disputes should be automatic and in prescribed form or
whether governments should leave themselves free to select such instruments as seem most likely to prove fruitful in the particular
case. Lastly in considering intervention, governments have to decide whether it should have the limited purpose of ensuring continuation of normal working or whether it should aim at resolving
the issues of the dispute.

The Instruments of Intervention and their Selection

The services of the state referred to in the last chapter will
not be further reviewed here, except to say that they are available
to precede, supplement or back up, the various forms of intervention
now to be considered, which may be summarised as:

a) Diplomacy
b) Public enquiry
c) Requirement to suspend action
d) Compulsory balloting

e) Compulsory arbitration
f) Public control or manning of operations
    i) assumption of direction
    ii) compulsory manning by existing workers
    iii) manning by state agents
g) Legislative settlement.

In practice diplomatic intervention, in the form of approaches by government officials to the parties, is likely to precede any other form of governmental action in serious labour disputes. It is a natural means to ascertain what is involved and what, if any, other forms of intervention may be useful.

The instrument of public enquiry works in two ways. The process of hearings at which the parties present their arguments to an experienced chairman, or panel, serves both to show the dispute in a new light to the parties and, by eliciting the circumstances, brings the pressure of public opinion to bear on them. To some extent it also injects an element of the public interest into negotiations. Those conducting the enquiry may make judgments on the issues involved, or formulate recommendations for their resolution, but merely to expose the facts of the situation can serve a useful purpose.

Two examples will serve to illustrate public enquiry. In the United Kingdom the Secretary for Employment has the power to set up a Court of Inquiry (which in no sense is a Court of Law). It is a power that has always been used sparingly. Courts of Inquiry are neither conciliators nor arbitrators and they have no power to enforce a settlement but as well as eliciting the facts they generally do make recommendations on which a reasonable settlement can be based. The Secretary also has powers to appoint a Committee of Investigation, a less formal body, whose report does not, as does that of a Court of Inquiry, have to be laid before Parliament. Under the recent extensive legislative changes in British industrial relations the Secretary has retained powers in respect of both kinds of body. Secondly, the United States Labor-Management Relations Act, 1947 (the Taft-Hartley Act), in a section dealing with disputes perilous to national health of safety, provides that when a national emergency procedure is invoked the first step is for the President to appoint a board of inquiry into the issue (though the board is not empowered to make recommendations for settlement).

A United States development worthy of note here applies to health care institutions. Amendments to the National Labor Relations Act in 1974 provide for appointment of a board of inquiry by the Director of the Federal Mediation and Conciliation Service if a threatened strike or lock out will substantially disrupt the delivery of health care in the locality concerned. The board is to make recommendations to settle the dispute. The amendments provide, in addition, for a 10-day notice before a strike or lock out may take place and a 15-day delay of such actions after a board of inquiry report issues.

Requirement to suspend action can also be exemplified by British and American experience. The short-lived (1971-1974) British Industrial Relations Act provided that in the case of a serious dispute the Secretary of State could obtain a Court Order for a 'cooling-off' period of up to 60 days. The Taft-Hartley Act, in the United States, provides that if, after receiving the findings of the board of inquiry, it appears that government intervention is justified, an injunction can be sought forbidding the parties to begin or continue the stoppage for an 80-day period. (If no settlement is reached at the end of 60 days the Board is required to make a further report on the current position of the parties and the efforts made for settlement). The concept underlying cooling-off provisions is that a breathing space is given during which conciliators can make fresh efforts to resolve the dispute. Additionally the parties themselves have time to have second thoughts which may lead towards a settlement. A distinction can be made between applying cooling-off orders where a contract has run out, so that no agreement on terms is in being (and workers may be unwilling to continue work) and the case in which there is a practice of extending the old contract, in which case a cooling-off requirement may be regarded as less of a challenge to the freedom to strike.

Both of the measures mentioned in the last paragraph also provided for compulsory balloting. Thus the British Industrial Relations Act enabled the Secretary to apply to the National Industrial Relations Court for an Order requiring a ballot of employees when he had reason to doubt, in a serious dispute, that industrial action had the support of the employees involved, whereupon such action should not be taken until the results of the ballot were known. In the United States, the Taft-Hartley Act requires that, between the 60th and 75th days of the cooling-off period, the National Labor Relations Board should ballot workers to find out if they are willing to accept the employer's last offer. Implicit in the idea of balloting is the belief that union leaders do not always reflect the true wishes of their membership and that a strike is a serious matter on which all concerned should have the opportunity to express their view (which they often, but by no means always, have under their union's rules). In fact, experience in both Britain, under the Industrial Relations Act, and in the United States suggests that union members are unlikely to vote against their leaders' policies in a government-initiated ballot. Even if they did so, by being destructive of the union's negotiating authority the result might be harmful to the long-term constructive relationship between parties.

Standing legislation providing for 'interest' disputes to be submitted to compulsory arbitration is rare in OECD countries in peacetime, except for certain classes of worker. However, as mentioned elsewhere, a conciliating/arbitrating body independent of the executive and dealing with disputes generally, is the central feature of the industrial relations system of Australia, the rationale for such a body being to provide a just means of resolving disputes without having to have recourse to industrial action, and being able to take account of the public interest. The Commissions' findings are binding but it is not obligatory to refer claims to them (in that sense the system is not really one of compulsory arbitration) and in fact the practice of collective bargaining outside the Commissions has been tending to grow. The hope that the Commissions' work would result in a low level of industrial action has not been fulfilled.

The main grounds of criticism of compulsory arbitration are firstly that it is destructive of the efforts which would otherwise be made by the parties to resolve their disputes, encouraging them to take relatively extreme positions; secondly that the parties may not agree with the assessment of the public interest as the arbitrators may want to take it into account; and, thirdly, that if the award is not to the liking of the parties they might, feeling no commitment to it, simply refuse to work under its terms.

Apart from these criticisms there is a common feeling that compulsion should only be used in very special situations, or for workers whose stoppages are particularly harmful to the public interest. In the latter context a novel form of arbitration is the procedure, known as 'Final Offer Selection'. The idea is that at the point of deadlock each party should put forward its final offer or offers. Mediation might follow but if the dispute remains unresolved the offers go forward to an arbitrator or arbitration board whereupon the offer regarded as the more reasonable - and only that offer - must be adopted as the binding settlement of the dispute; the arbitration may be either on an item-by-item or on a "package" basis. It has been argued that such a procedure discourages the parties from taking unreasonable positions and affords a basis of settlement in terms already discussed by the parties. Against Final Offer Selection it has been argued that the arbitrator is forced into deciding options which are not at all acceptable to one of the parties and that it is difficult to arrive at a workable settlement in what may be an extremely complex dispute. Whatever the balance of these

arguments it is a fact that the idea of Final Offer Selection has
not 'caught on' and its use is limited to some groups of public
employees, often police or firefighters, mainly in the United States.
Where used, however, it seems to have been quite successful.(1)
Another procedure of interest in this context is "Mediation-
Arbitration", whereby the parties agree in advance that the mediator
of issues between them should become an arbitrator for all issues
unresolved by mediation.

Public control or manning of operations takes a variety of
forms. Its least interventionary form is the partial operation of
essential services, whereby certain workers are designated, by the
parties or by the government, to continue working under existing conditions to provide just enough goods or services to relieve the emergency conditions. It is not, of course, easy to decide the basis for
such operation and the union(s) concerned may well feel that it
impairs their bargaining strength unreasonably. Nevertheless, partial operation has worked with some success in Belgium and has been
discussed in both New Zealand and the United States. It should be
added that partial operation goes further than the arrangement, common to many disputes, where the parties themselves make provision
for vital maintenance work and work for hospitals, etc. to continue
during a dispute.

Of a somewhat different nature is an old idea, scarcely ever
used in practice, the 'non-stoppage' or 'statutory strike', when the
intending strikers continue to work while each of the parties suffers
agreed financial penalties until such time as a settlement is made.
Though underlying contest of economic power remains, it seems unlikely that a procedure of this kind could operate without full support from the parties and its use in a bitter, major dispute is
improbable.

A second form of public direction is exemplified by the concept
of 'seizure', under which strikers are required to continue work under the prevailing conditions, with the government assuming control
of operations (and profits if any), until agreement can be reached
between the parties. Such a drastic procedure would seem unaccept-
able in many societies and it does not seem to have been used in
recent years.

Thirdly, a government may enforce continuation of essential work
by conscripting strikers into state service, making them subject to
military discipline, as M. Briand did in the French railway strike
of 1910, and, more recently, as the Spanish authorities did with

1) See, for instance, J.L. Stern, et al. Final-Offer Arbitration:
The Effects on Public Safety Employee Bargaining, Lexington
Books - D.C. Heath, Lexington, 1975.

striking railway and post office workers in January 1976. Such a practice has always been considered exceptional.

A government may also safeguard essential services by using troops - for example to unload perishable foodstuffs in a dock strike; to provide a rudimentary public transport network in a transport strike or to clear uncollected garbage. Governments have normally been most reluctant to intervene in this way but have found it necessary to do so in exceptional circumstances.

Lastly, there have been cases where governments have felt compelled to legislate (or threaten to legislate, which has sometimes brought about agreement between the parties) a return to work or even terms of a return to work. Examples have been the Swedish senior public employees' dispute of 1971 and the two-year national wage settlement imposed on both public and private sectors in Denmark in March 1975. In Canada, although the parliaments have legislated returns to work, usually they do not legislate on the terms for such a return, delegating this responsibility to an independent arbitrator or arbitration board. Normally, however, the processes of legislation are too slow and too insensitive to the nuances of industrial usage for the method to be used frequently. Additionally, unless it is carefully attuned to the needs and attitudes of employers and workers both parties may feel resentment and be reluctant to operate under the settlement.

Three particular aspects of disputes remain to be discussed, namely national wage disputes, disputes concerning public employees, and the problems of enforcement.

Chapter 4

SOME PARTICULAR PROBLEM AREAS

1. National Wage Disputes

It was rare before World War II for governments in most OECD
countries to become involved in wage negotiations. Subsequently,
however, and notably in the 1970s, the determination of wages (as of
prices and other incomes) came to be so important in relation to national economic policy-making that most governments could no longer
ignore what happened in major wage negotiations. The problems that
beset this relationship have been discussed in other OECD work(1) and
some of the instruments available to governments to deal with particularly obdurate situations are outlined earlier in this Report. None
of this need be repeated here but it is appropriate to point to the
extent to which, in a very few years, governments have found it necessary to intervene in bargaining on account of the wider implications of its outcome. Governmental steps have ranged from strict
wage control measures to the achievement of wide-ranging agreements
between governments, trade unions and employers. To illustrate,
apart from the Danish case mentioned above, one can cite the
Netherlands Act of 1970, permitting the government to interfere with
the terms and conditions of specific collective agreements (though an
assurance was given that the power would only be used sparingly). In
another case the Irish Government, in 1975, called on the unions and
employers to renegotiate a recently concluded central national
agreement.

2. Disputes in Public Employment

Another area in which conflict has increased, at least in some
countries, and in which new modes of settlement have had to be evolved is public service employment. The area is not easy to define
and varies from country to country, though a rule-of-thumb definition could be that a public servant or employee is one whose emolu-
ments are, for practical purposes, directly dependent on decisions
made by the government, or a regional or local authority. Taken to

1) Notably in Socially Responsible Wages Policies and Inflation,
   OECD, Paris, 1975.

41

include publicly owned industries the numbers covered may amount to well over a quarter of the employed population in a country and public employment has been growing in almost every Member country.

Basically three broad different groups of public servants and employees may be distinguished: the civil servants who carry out the administration of the state (and, perhaps with different conditions, directly employed 'industrial' workers); those who serve regional or local authorities; and workers in publicly owned or controlled services or industrial undertakings, including workers in public utilities. At least some of these groups have traditionally been regarded as self-contained entities in which privileged conditions, such as security of employment and pensions, and other better-than-average conditions prevailed. The circumstances were such that there was little propensity for militancy.

But, as has been noted above, there has been a considerable increase in labour conflict in public employment - at least in some Member countries. Strikes are nothing new in publicly-owned industry but the last few years have seen appreciable industrial action by hitherto generally peaceful groups, including teachers, police and firemen, doctors, postmen, air traffic controllers, and local government employees; even by administrative workers in civil services. The discontent of these groups may be attributed in part to the general causes of industrial tension described in Chapter 1 but there are other reasons. A major one has been apparent erosion of comparative advantage, as manual workers and others have achieved improved conditions, be it through collective bargaining, legislated improvements or through progressive taxation. Public employees have often found it necessary to press their case strongly for not being left out in the scramble to keep pace with inflation. The processes of organisational decision-making have sometimes made it frustratingly difficult for them to locate the real source of authority on wages and working conditions and to engage in meaningful bargaining; also, some have felt that the modes by which their conditions are regulated are ill-suited to the 1970s. It may be added that in several countries unionisation is appreciably higher in the public than in the private sectors.

In many Member countries some of these newly militant groups work under public law and not under contracts of employment and in some countries they do not enjoy the right to bargain collectively or to strike (though this has not always prevented their having recourse to strike action - without prescribed sanctions being imposed on them). The view is commonly held that if, in the public interest, workers are expected not to strike they should be compensated by its being assured that they should have no grounds for complaint, but this has not always been felt to operate by those concerned.

Two particular arguments are used against freedom to strike on the part of public employees. One is that such a strike would be more in the nature of disobedience to a democratically elected government - and hence an attack on the community at large - than it is an industrial dispute; the other, that the strikers are people who carry out the essential business of the state, which must not be impeded. The first of these arguments, resting on notions of sovereignty, is becoming increasingly difficult to reconcile with reality, as the points of difference between public and other employees become fewer. Also, the argument fails to distinguish between government's role as guardian of the nation's affairs and its role as an employer. It can also be argued that part of the essence of sovereignty is that it includes the power to share authority. The argument has been abandoned by some countries, which have provided that nearly all public employees should have the same rights as those in the private sector. Other countries have achieved much the same result by adopting what are virtually bargaining processes, the outcomes of which are put to the legislature for formal approval. The second argument about public sector disputes is rather more practical and even in countries where public employees generally enjoy similar rights to those in the private sector some exceptions may be made, though it is sometimes difficult to draw the line. (In one Member country employees tending the greenhouse of the Head of State's representative were reported as classified among those vital to the public interest).

The tendency has been towards narrowing the definition of those whose continuous work is essential to the community. As a senior ILO official has pointed out they are likely to "include certain high-level government administrators, certain members of the police force, senior officers of the armed forces and certain key personnel in hospitals, fire brigades and similar services". Others, he concludes, "are likely to be assimilated to employees in the private sector".(1)

In the public as in the private sector, distinction is frequently made between disputes of rights and disputes of interests. Machinery for adjusting 'rights' disputes has long been common: for the most part machinery for dealing with disputes concerning wages and conditions, which are most frequently at the root of strikes in the public as in the private sector, is newer. Most of the aids to industrial peace used in the private sector are also found in the public sector, despite the complicating factor of the sovereignty

---

1) J.S. Schregle, 'Labour Relations in the Public Sector' in International Labour Review, Vol. 110, No. 5, November, 1974.

concept, which comes up where, for instance, a third party adjudicates between a government and its employees. Fact finding, conciliation, mediation and arbitration, sometimes compulsory arbitration, are all in use in various countries. There have been cases of legislative intervention and maintenance of services by military forces. In some countries special peacemaking machinery exists for the public service.

As in private industry it is now common to find joint bodies, of various forms, concerned with conditions in public service. Thus Canada has a Public Services Staff Relations Board (and provides an option for workers to choose between conciliation plus the right to strike and arbitration without the right to strike - the strike option route being increasingly favoured). Finland has a Public Services Disputes Committee; Sweden a Public Service Council, and the United States, for certain questions concerning Federal employees, a Federal Services Impasse Panel, some States having similar institutions. The United Kingdom has its 'Whitley' machinery, established after the First World War, and has a more recent Pay Research Unit which assesses bases of comparison with private industry.

It seems likely that public service disputes will grow in importance in a number of countries and it seems important that satisfactory machinery should exist to deal with them. In this connection it may be noted that the International Labour Conference, 1977, is considering "Freedom of association and procedures for determining conditions of employment in the public service".(1)

3.   The Problem of Enforcement

Third and last, in this review of particular aspects of labour disputes, is the problem of enforcement of laws and agreements.

The value of 'peace' clauses in procedural agreements has already been discussed, albeit briefly, in Chapter 2. The problem to be outlined here is that where workers put themselves in breach of legislation, or of a decision by a court of law, in a manner for which penalties are provided. It may be difficult for the enforcing authority to take action in some such cases. There may well be a feeling that in human terms the merits of a particular case lie with the strikers rather than the law. It may be politically wiser to

1) Problems in the public service have had considerable attention in the ILO in recent years. See, for example, the Reports of the Technical Conference on the Public Service (Geneva 1975) and Reports VII(1) and VII(2) on Freedom of Association and Procedures for Determining Conditions in the Public Service (Geneva, 1976 and 1977).

ignore the situation than to impose penalties. Unfair as it may seem, if there is no public feeling on the issue and the numbers are small it may be that no problem will arise from imposing a penalty whereas if several thousands of workers are involved and public feeling is high it is another matter.

Some countries (e.g. Denmark and Sweden) have legislated in recent years to remove penalties from certain strikes. In some countries no question is raised about the justice of penalties. But though several countries retain, in one form or other, fairly general machinery for penalising strikers and/or their organisations for action held to be unlawful, there has been an increasing tendency for sanctions to be challenged, frequently successfully. There have been notable cases in Australia, Canada, Ireland and the United Kingdom, for example.

Having regard to the wide variation in the provisions for dealing with labour disputes in countries with different legal and social traditions, uniformity of treatment as regards sanctions cannot be expected but changing attitudes in a number of countries suggest that it is well to ensure that existing provisions still reflect public will and need.

It may be useful to add that much of what has been said above about strikes and the law is equally relevant to the subject of picketing, in which practice has also been tending to become more permissive in some countries.

SUMMARY - CONCLUSIONS

As made clear at the outset the objective of this Report has not been to present an encyclopaedic account of labour disputes but a perspective on them as they appear today. To meet even this limited objective in a short report it has been necessary to forego almost all consideration of the important legal aspects, of disputes concerning individual grievances, and of 'rights' disputes. The focus has been on collective 'interests' disputes, and how they are dealt with. The Report has adopted the general standpoints that the right to strike is a fundamental freedom; that disputes are by no means to be regarded as intrinsically bad; but that peaceful means of avoiding or resolving them are normally preferable to "battling it out".

The picture that emerges does not suggest that there have been any great overall changes in the volume or nature of disputes, nor much change in the relativities between high-dispute and low-dispute countries. Looked at globally, after a generally peaceful period in the '50s and '60s (and in several countries a sharp increase around 1968-1971), the volume of conflict tended to rise and, when it fell, with the onset of recession, to stay above the levels common in the previous 20 years or so. The issues in disputes tended to become more varied but, most notably, the proportion of the population backing their claims with industrial action increased considerably. Negotiations concerning wages came to have increased significance for governmental economic and social policies, so that many governments become involved in incomes policies, and in some countries special difficulties were encountered in respect of public employees. Though there is no clear indication of future trends, sources of tension in employment seem more likely to increase than decrease.

There appears to be widespread agreement across countries that wherever possible unions and employers should resolve their disputes themselves. The many levels and variety of ways in which they can do so were too complex to be detailed in this Report. It seems clear that more could be done, in many countries, through improved managerial practices, and speedy and effective negotiating procedures, to reduce the incidence of disputes.

The role of the State in relation to disputes is seen as a difficult one in most countries, and as of increasing importance. It is the more difficult in those cases where the State may have to satisfy a triple responsibility at the same time - as guardian of the economy, as employer, and as conciliator. It is of increasing importance to governments because of growing interdependencies, so that disputes seem to have wider and wider impact on the public and because the State itself is employing more and more people. The role of the State, while differing according to the traditions of each country, lies primarily within the fields of establishing minimum standards; of setting 'ground rules' for the handling of disputes by the parties; of providing information and advice; of affording conciliation, mediation, arbitration and fact-finding facilities; and of acting in the public interest where a dispute seems likely to prove seriously damaging to the nation. Additionally, of course, the State is concerned with disputes in its capacity as employer.

Though the volume and nature of labour disputes do not at present constitute a serious national problem outside a small number of Member countries, few countries have grounds for complacency. Much could be done to make for smoother working of industrial relations systems, and the conflictual aspects of operating income policies, and of public employment, in particular, call for attention.

Time has produced few useful new techniques for dealing with disputes but the considerable variety of institutions and practices to be found suggests that, with due regard to the differences between national systems and traditions, and to the problems inevitably associated with transplantation, there is much that countries can learn from the experience of others.

Industrial action is one of the means whereby adaptations are brought about in our societies and tensions released and in this sense can be a source of social advance and - paradoxically - of social stability. It can even be argued that there are circumstances where the absence of strikes is harmful, where, for instance, deep resentment is built up among workers but instead of being cleared through open conflict expresses itself through alienation and inefficient operation; or where managements make concession after concession to avoid disruption of production, at the expense of long-term efficiency.

But, whether or not the outcome of a dispute is desirable, industrial action remains a costly means of resolving grievances or achieving social advance. What more satisfactory ways can be found to give desirable results at less cost?

The first, rather obvious, point to make is that prevention (by reducing causes of dispute, not by suppressing dissatisfaction) is better than cure. The case histories of particular disputes suggest that more sensitivity on the part of management towards the human side of enterprise, more effective personnel administration, and sometimes a more co-operative approach on the part of workers, could considerably reduce unnecessary disputes.

It is also evident that in a number of countries national and regional collective bargaining and consultative institutions and practices do not function as well as they might.(1) National level reviews of procedures used by employers and their organisations and trade unions might have a usefully stimulative effect in such cases.

Amongst the ways in which the State can facilitate adoption of effective machinery for handling disputes are educational programmes, informational and advisory services, and industrial relations research. But more important, in most countries, are the State's provision of conciliation, mediation and arbitration services for the parties, and the use of personal diplomacy. The form and extent of such services will depend on the extent to which employers and unions satisfactorily regulate their own affairs and, more generally, on national traditions and administrative structures. Two general questions have to be considered in relation to such services - their degree of autonomy and their powers. If they are to be regarded as neutral, as they must if they are to be trusted by the parties, and particularly if they are to be of use in respect of part of the public sector, they should be as independent as possible of administrative departments of government. It does not follow that the services should be free to ignore governmental economic policies but independence does give them greater flexibility, even in this area. It further seems useful if unions and employers themselves are closely associated with the management of such agencies.

Powers of compulsion change mediatory institutions from available services to authoritative agencies - and at present the value of compulsory arbitration seems limited. As to powers of intervention, on the other hand, no one would wish to endow these bodies with inquisitorial powers to use as they wish, but it seems reasonable that they should be enabled to offer their services where a dispute has broken out, or seems likely, and that government should be able to make use of them to intervene in disputes which are of appreciable public concern.

Powers of enquiry may be associated with fact finding and bringing the circumstances to public attention - with or without recommendations for settlement. It seems that, by enlisting the force of

1) For an analysis of the relationship between strikes and procedures, see Clegg, op. cit., Chapter 6.

public opinion, an independent public enquiry can make a valuable contribution to settling disputes. The very process of enquiry tends to bring about a shift in the attitudes of the disputants. Also, any recommendations that are made have a certain moral force and even if one or both of the parties be reluctant to accept them, they may provide a constructive basis for further negotiation.

Independent enquiry and fact finding can be particularly useful in disputes having a substantial effect on the community. Though the process of enquiry may take some time, the disputants are commonly willing to continue normal working until the results of the intervention are known.

The use of compulsory independent ballots on whether to take industrial action does not seem to have been very successful and adds to the evidence that any legal powers available to governments to use such ballots should only be activated if there is a clear probability that the result will be constructive.

Use of the toughest instruments of the State - seizure, conscription, use of defence forces, legislation, etc. - is likely to be a matter for political judgment in the light of the degree of public support for firm governmental action and of the opposition that may be expected. But it is clear that such instruments should only be used when a dispute is seriously affecting the life of the nation.

"Seriously affecting the life of the nation" imports questions of judgment. Several laws and agreements endeavour to define (though rarely with any precision) the kinds of dispute in question, speaking of such matters as 'national health and safety', 'disturbing essential public services', or 'services or enterprises regarded as indispensable to provide for the needs of the nation'. Other countries are able to take action under emergency powers.

In our ever more closely integrated societies, and with a wider variety of workers taking strike action, disputes "seriously affecting the life of the nation" have come to be more common - and may come to be more common still. However, it seems doubtful that they could be defined with any precision, or indeed that closer definition would be particularly useful.

Where wage bargaining is centralised, governments will continue to face the possibility of widespread conflict should negotiations finally break down. Experience offers no panacea for such problems, each needing to be dealt with according to its circumstances. Perhaps the most that can be said by way of generalisation is that intervention is likely to be more constructive at an earlier, more flexible, stage than when actual breakdown occurs.

Though many countries still have few problems arising from public employment, disputes in this sector will probably become more important and the differences between the terms of employment prevailing in the private and the public sectors seem likely to decrease. Apart from ensuring sound personnel policies in the public sector, governments may do well to review the basis of industrial relations in that sector.

In responding to the challenge of labour disputes governments have a wide choice of 'standing' and 'ad hoc' instruments which they can use. Given the variability of the circumstances of disputes it seems important to maintain a wide variety and, further, that governments should not confine themselves to automatic invocation of particular instruments in particular circumstances. The parties should know what public services are available to them but at the point at which intervention in the public interest must be considered governments need flexibility for devising the most constructive approach to make to the dispute.

Many of the statements made in this Report do not fit the circumstances of all Member countries, particularly those countries where disputes are few, where formal state machinery for dealing with collective 'interests' disputes has not been considered appropriate, or where the weight of third party involvement in disputes rests with quasi-judicial institutions, rather than with the administration. Nevertheless, the forces underlying present trends in industrial relations systems are common to nearly all Member countries, though they may express themselves in different ways.

Aaron B. and Wedderburn K.W. (Eds.) - Industrial Conflict: A Comparative Legal Survey, Longman, London, 1972.

Aaron B. (Ed) - Dispute Settlement Procedures in Five Western European Countries, University of California, Los Angeles, 1969.

Aaron B. (Ed) - Labour Courts and Grievance Settlement in Western Europe, University of California, Berkeley, 1971.

Barkin, S. (Ed) - Worker Militancy and its Consequences, 1965-75, Praeger, New York, 1975.

Blanpain, R. - Prevention and Settlement of Collective Labour Disputes in the EEC Countries, in Industrial Law Journal, June and September, 1972.

Dahrendorf, R. - Class and Class Conflict in Industrial Society, Routledge and Kegan Paul, London, 1959.

Dufty, N.F. - Changes in Labour-Management Relations in the Enterprise, OECD, Paris, 1975.

Fisher, M. - Measurement of Labour Disputes and their Economic Effects, OECD, Paris, 1973.

de Givry, J. - Labour Courts as Channels for the Settlement of Labour Disputes; an International Review, in British Journal of Industrial Relations, November, 1968.

de Givry, J. and Schregle, J. - The Role of the Third Party in the Settlement of Grievances at the Plant Level, in Roberts, B.C. (Ed) Industrial Relations: Contemporary Issues, Macmillan, London, 1968.

Goetz - Girey, R. - Le Mouvement des Grèves en France, Sirey, Paris, 1965.

Hyman, R. - Strikes, Fontana/Collins, London, 1972.

Ingham, G.K. - Strikes and Industrial Conflict, Britain and Scandinavia, Macmillan, London, 1974.

Kahn Freund, O. (Ed) - Labour Relations and the Law, Stevens, London, 1965.

Kahn Freund, O. - Labour and the Law, Stevens, London, 1972.

Kahn Freund, O. and Hepple, B. - Laws Against Strikes, Fabian Society, London, 1972.

Knowles, K.G.J.C. - Strikes, Blackwell, Oxford, 1952.

Kornhauser, A., Dublin, R. and Ross, A.M. (Eds) - Industrial Conflict, McGraw/Hill, New York, 1954.

Livernash, E.R. - Collective Bargaining in the Basic Steel Industry. A study of the Public Interest and the Role of Government, Greenwood, Westport, Connecticut, 1976 (reprint of a 1961 report).

Oxnam, D.W. - Issues in Industrial Conflict: An International Comparison, in Journal of Industrial Relations, June, 1971.

Pettman, Barrie O. - Strikes. A Selected Bibliography, MCB Books, Bradford, 1976.

Ross, A.M. and Hartman, P.T. - Changing Patterns of Industrial Conflict, Wiley, New York, 1960.

Schregle, J. - Labour Relations in the Public Sector, in International Labour Review, November, 1974.

Snyder, D. - Institutional Setting and Industrial Conflict: Comparative Analyses of France, Italy and the United States, in American Sociological Review, June, 1975.

Sociologie du Travail: Issue 2/71: (Special Number) Conflits sociaux et transformations des relations professionnelles en Italie et en France, Paris, 1971.

Spitaels, G. (Ed) - Les Conflits Sociaux en Europe, Marabout, Brussels, 1971.

Turner, H.A. - Is Britain Really Strike-Prone? Department of Applied Economics, Occasional Papers No. 20, Cambridge University Press, Cambridge, 1969.

Wigham, E. - Strikes and the Government, 1893-1974, Macmillan, London, 1976.

and particularly:

Adam G. and Bachy J-P. - The Services of the State in the Resolution of Labour Disputes, 1976. (mimeographed document).

Baker, K. - Emergency Disputes, 1973; (mimeographed document).

Shalev, M. - Trends in Employment Conflict, 1976. (mimeographed document).

OECD SALES AGENTS
DÉPOSITAIRES DES PUBLICATIONS DE L'OCDE

ARGENTINA – ARGENTINE
Carlos Hirsch S.R.L., Florida 165,
BUENOS-AIRES, Tel. 33-1787-2391 Y 30-7122

AUSTRALIA – AUSTRALIE
Australia & New Zealand Book Company Pty Ltd.,
23 Cross Street, (P.O.B. 459)
BROOKVALE NSW 2100   Tel. 938-2244

AUSTRIA – AUTRICHE
Gerold and Co., Graben 31, WIEN 1. Tel. 52.22.35

BELGIUM – BELGIQUE
LCLS
44 rue Otlet, B 1070 BRUXELLES .Tel. 02-521 28 13

BRAZIL – BRÉSIL
Mestre Jou S.A., Rua Guaipá 518,
Caixa Postal 24090, 05089 SAO PAULO 10. Tel. 261-1920
Rua Senador Dantas 19 s/205-6, RIO DE JANEIRO GB.
Tel. 232-07. 32

CANADA
Renouf Publishing Company Limited,
2182 St. Catherine Street West,
MONTREAL, Quebec H3H 1M7 Tel. (514) 937-3519

DENMARK – DANEMARK
Munksgaards Boghandel,
Nørregade 6, 1165 KØBENHAVN K. Tel. (01) 12 85 70

FINLAND – FINLANDE
Akateeminen Kirjakauppa
Keskuskatu 1, 00100 HELSINKI 10. Tel. 625.901

FRANCE
Bureau des Publications de l'OCDE,
2 rue André-Pascal, 75775 PARIS CEDEX 16. Tel. (1) 524.81.67
Principal correspondant :
13602 AIX-EN-PROVENCE : Librairie de l'Université.
Tel. 26.18.08

GERMANY – ALLEMAGNE
Alexander Horn,
D - 6200 WIESBADEN, Spiegelgasse 9
Tel. (6121) 37-42-12

GREECE – GRÈCE
Librairie Kauffmann, 28 rue du Stade,
ATHÈNES 132. Tel. 322.21.60

HONG-KONG
Government Information Services,
Sales and Publications Office, Beaconsfield House, 1st floor,
Queen's Road, Central.   Tel. H-233191

ICELAND – ISLANDE
Snaebjörn Jónsson and Co., h.f.,
Hafnarstraeti 4 and 9, P.O.B. 1131, REYKJAVIK.
Tel. 13133/14281/11936

INDIA – INDE
Oxford Book and Stationery Co.:
NEW DELHI, Scindia House. Tel. 45896
CALCUTTA, 17 Park Street. Tel.240832

ITALY – ITALIE
Libreria Commissionaria Sansoni:
Via Lamarmora 45, 50121 FIRENZE. Tel. 579751
Via Bartolini 29, 20155 MILANO. Tel. 365083
Sub-depositari:
Editrice e Libreria Herder,
Piazza Montecitorio 120, 00 186 ROMA. Tel. 674628
Libreria Hoepli, Via Hoepli 5, 20121 MILANO. Tel. 865446
Libreria Lattes, Via Garibaldi 3, 10122 TORINO. Tel. 519274
La diffusione delle edizioni OCSE è inoltre assicurata dalle migliori
librerie nelle città più importanti.

JAPAN – JAPON
OECD Publications and Information Center
Akasaka Park Building, 2-3-4 Akasaka, Minato-ku,
TOKYO 107. Tel. 586-2016

KOREA - CORÉE
Pan Korea Book Corporation,
P.O.Box nº 101 Kwangwhamun, SÉOUL. Tel. 72-7369

LEBANON – LIBAN
Documenta Scientifica/Redico,
Edison Building, Bliss Street, P.O.Box 5641, BEIRUT.
Tel. 354429–344425

MEXICO & CENTRAL AMERICA
Centro de Publicaciones de Organismos Internacionales S.A.,
Av. Chapultepec 345, Apartado Postal 6-981
MEXICO 6, D.F. Tel. 533-45-09

THE NETHERLANDS – PAYS-BAS
Staatsuitgeverij
Chr. Plantijnstraat
'S-GRAVENHAGE. Tel. 070-814511
Voor bestellingen: Tel. 070-624551

NEW ZEALAND – NOUVELLE-ZÉLANDE
The Publications Manager,
Government Printing Office,
WELLINGTON: Mulgrave Street (Private Bag),
World Trade Centre, Cubacade, Cuba Street,
Rutherford House, Lambton Quay, Tel. 737-320
AUCKLAND: Rutland Street (P.O.Box 5344), Tel. 32.919
CHRISTCHURCH: 130 Oxford Tce (Private Bag), Tel. 50.331
HAMILTON: Barton Street (P.O.Box 857), Tel. 80.103
DUNEDIN: T & G Building, Princes Street (P.O.Box 1104),
Tel. 78.294

NORWAY – NORVÈGE
Johan Grundt Tanums Bokhandel,
Karl Johansgate 41/43, OSLO 1. Tel. 02-332980

PAKISTAN
Mirza Book Agency, 65 Shahrah Quaid-E-Azam, LAHORE 3.
Tel. 66839

PHILIPPINES
R.M. Garcia Publishing House, 903 Quezon Blvd. Ext.,
QUEZON CITY, P.O.Box 1860 – MANILA. Tel. 99.98.47

PORTUGAL
Livraria Portugal, Rua do Carmo 70-74, LISBOA 2. Tel. 360582/3

SPAIN – ESPAGNE
Mundi-Prensa Libros, S.A.
Castelló 37, Apartado 1223, MADRID-1. Tel. 275.46.55
Libreria Bastinos, Pelayo, 52, BARCELONA 1. Tel. 222.06.00

SWEDEN – SUÈDE
AB CE Fritzes Kungl Hovbokhandel,
Box 16 356, S 103 27 STH, Regeringsgatan 12,
DS STOCKHOLM. Tel. 08/23 89 00

SWITZERLAND – SUISSE
Librairie Payot, 6 rue Grenus, 1211 GENÈVE 11. Tel. 022-31.89.50

TAIWAN – FORMOSE
National Book Company,
84-5 Sing Sung Rd., Sec. 3, TAIPEI 107. Tel. 321.0698

UNITED KINGDOM – ROYAUME-UNI
H.M. Stationery Office, P.O.B. 569,
LONDON SEI 9 NH. Tel. 01-928-6977, Ext. 410 or
49 High Holborn, LONDON WC1V 6 HB (personal callers)
Branches at: EDINBURGH, BIRMINGHAM, BRISTOL,
MANCHESTER, CARDIFF, BELFAST.

UNITED STATES OF AMERICA
OECD Publications and Information Center, Suite 1207,
1750 Pennsylvania Ave., N.W. WASHINGTON, D.C.20006.
Tel. (202)724-1857

VENEZUELA
Libreria del Este, Avda. F. Miranda 52, Edificio Galipán,
CARACAS 106. Tel. 32 23 01/33 26 04/33 24 73

YUGOSLAVIA – YOUGOSLAVIE
Jugoslovenska Knjiga, Terazije 27, P.O.B. 36, BEOGRAD.
Tel. 621-992

Les commandes provenant de pays où l'OCDE n'a pas encore désigné de dépositaire peuvent être adressées à :
OCDE, Bureau des Publications, 2 rue André-Pascal, 75775 PARIS CEDEX 16.
Orders and inquiries from countries where sales agents have not yet been appointed may be sent to:
OECD, Publications Office, 2 rue André-Pascal, 75775 PARIS CEDEX 16.

OECD PUBLICATIONS
2, rue André-Pascal, 75775 Paris Cedex 16

No. 40.947 1978

PRINTED IN FRANCE

DATE DUE

MAY 1 7 1991			